PRE-SCHOOL PRE-NUMBER SKILLS

Fun-filled Activities

An imprint of Om Books International

Big

In each set, circle (O) the one that is **big**.

Small

Small

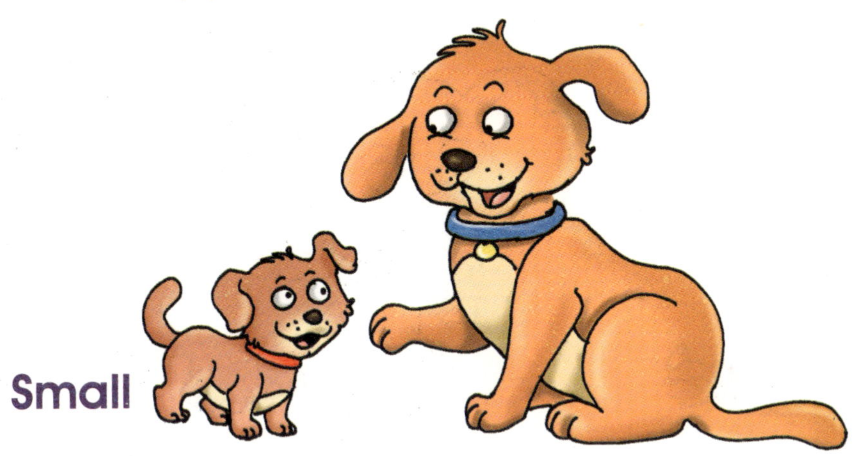

In each set circle (O) the one that is **small**.

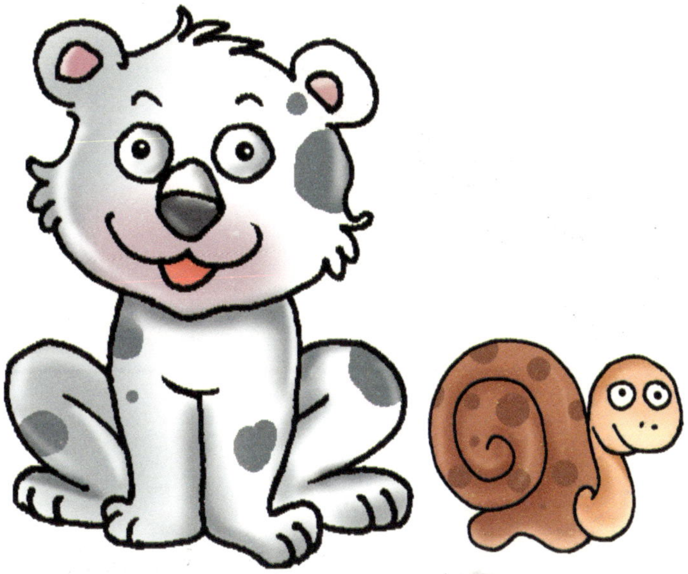

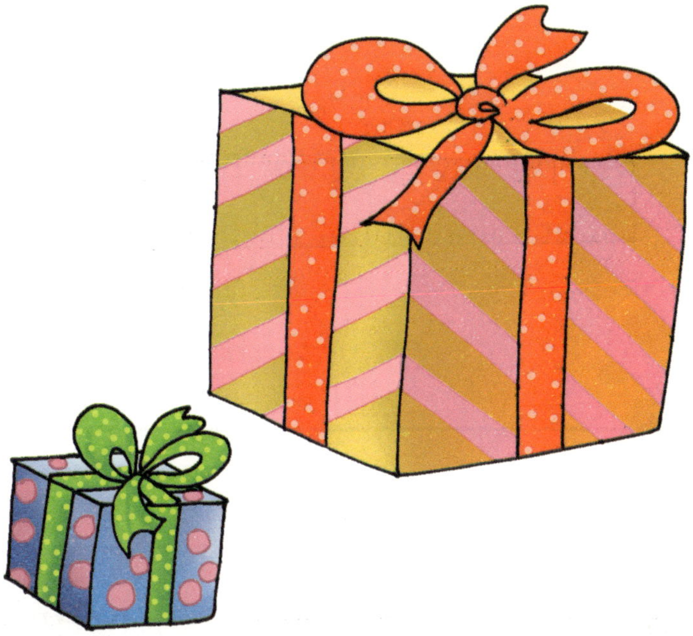

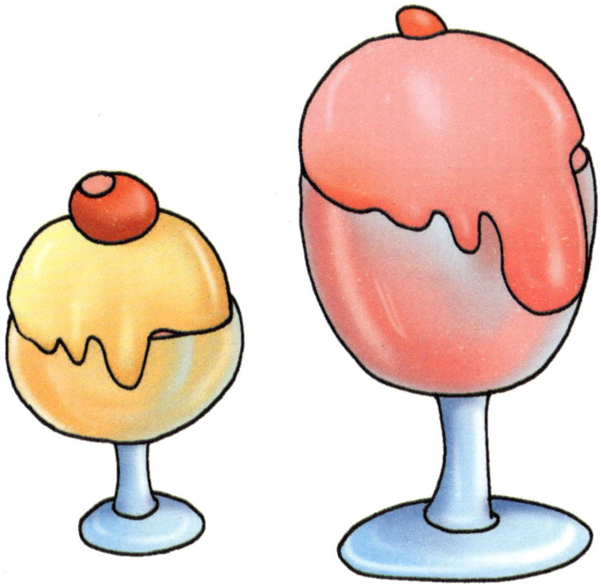

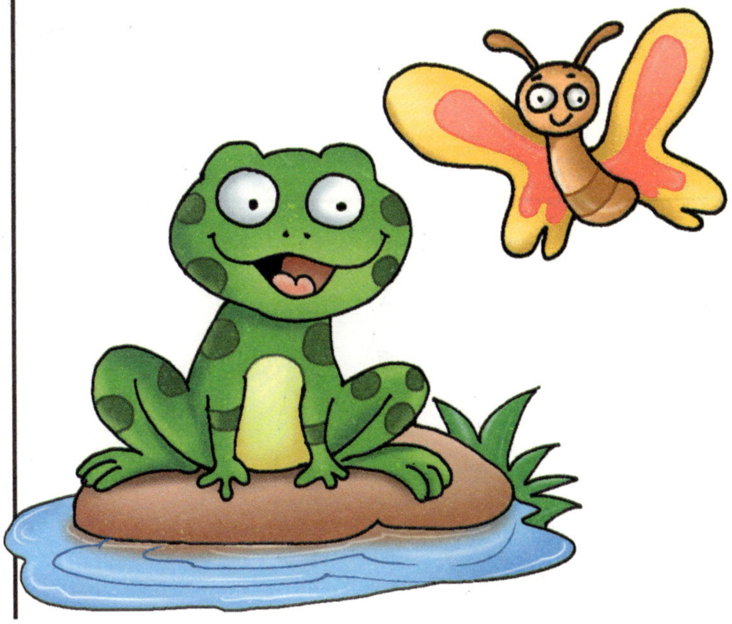

Long

Long Nose

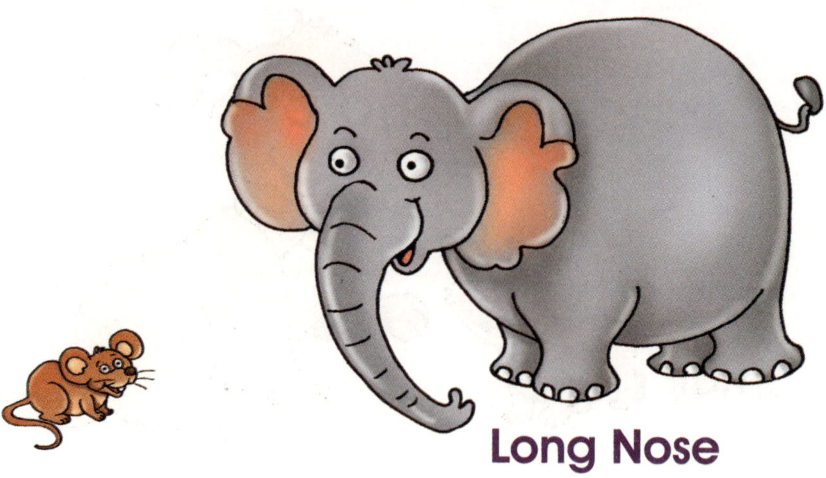

Tick (✓) the **longer** one in each row.

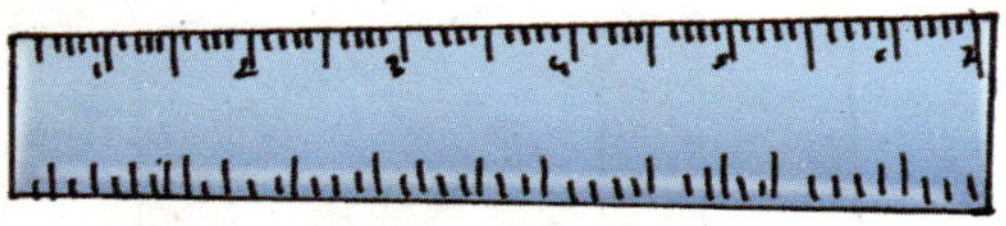

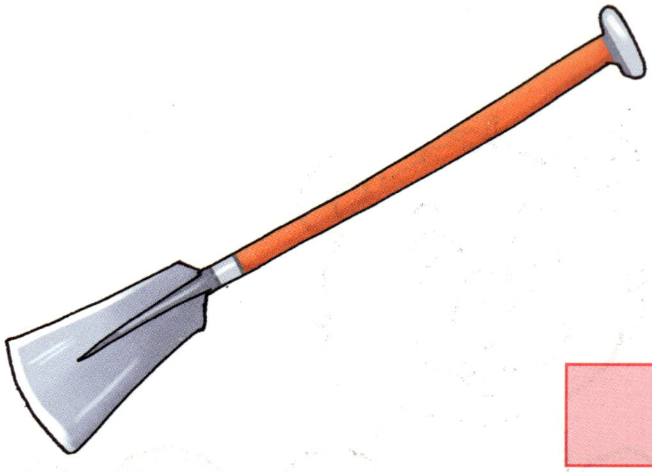

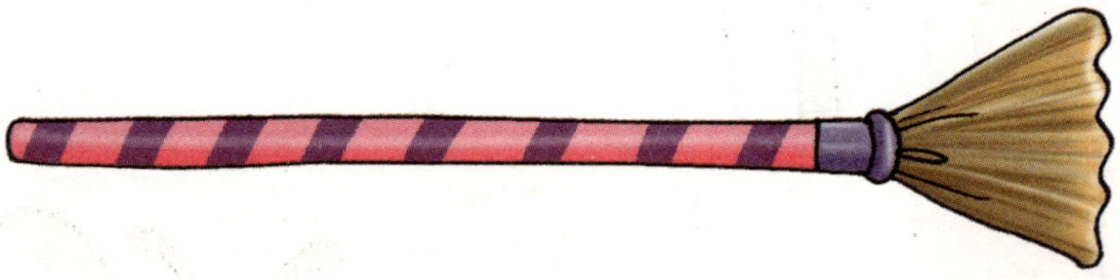

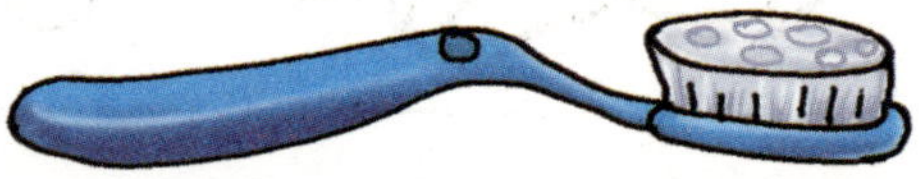

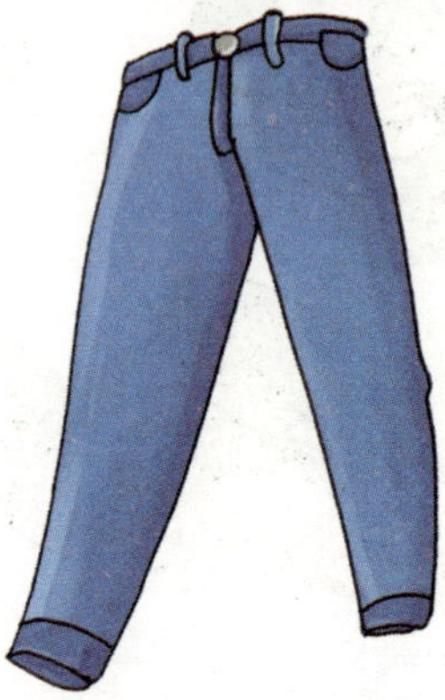

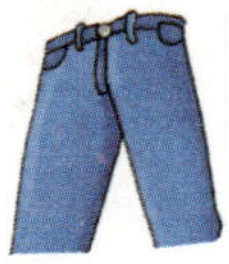

Short

Put a cross (×) for the **shorter** one in each row.

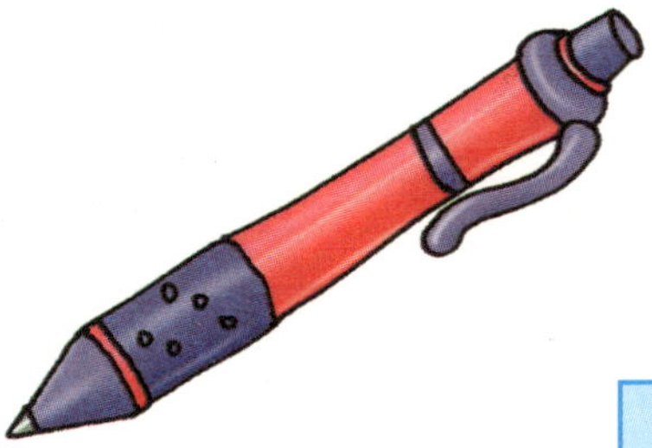

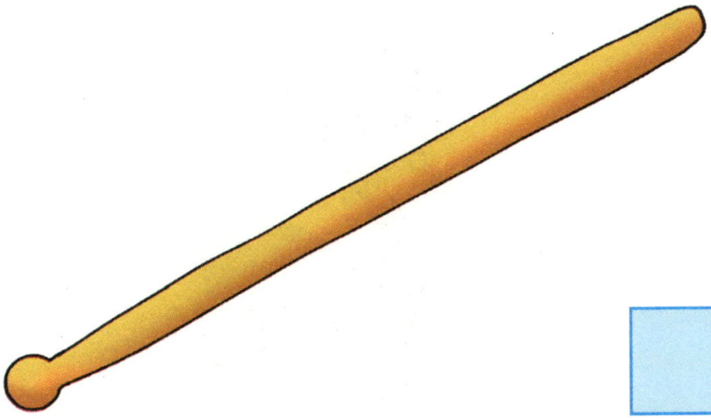

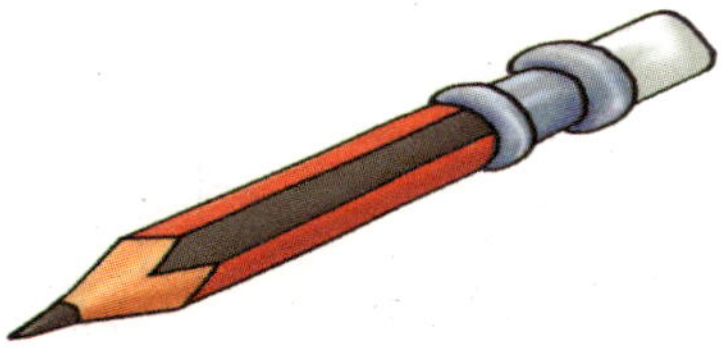

Tall

Circle (O) the one that is **tall** in each row.

Short

Circle (O) all the animals that are **shorter** than the man.

Thick

This tree is **thick**.

In each row, tick (✓) the picture that is **thick**.

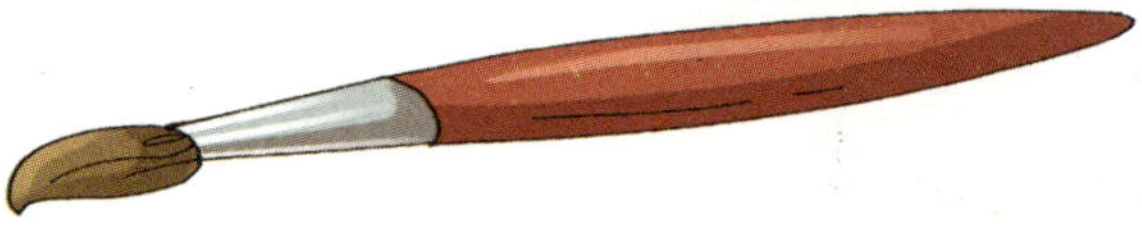

Thin

This pole is **thin**.

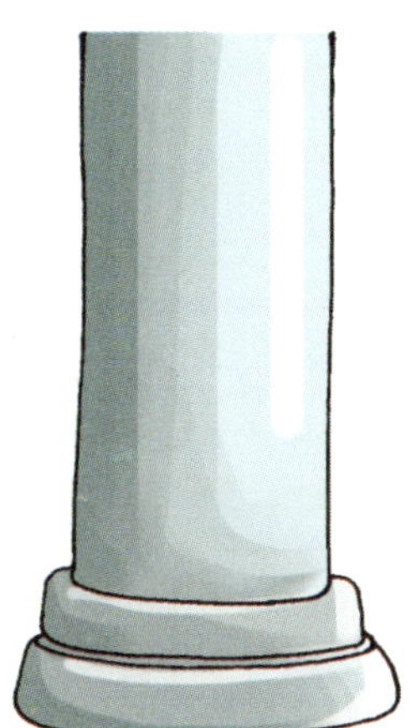

In each row, circle (O) the picture that is **thin**.

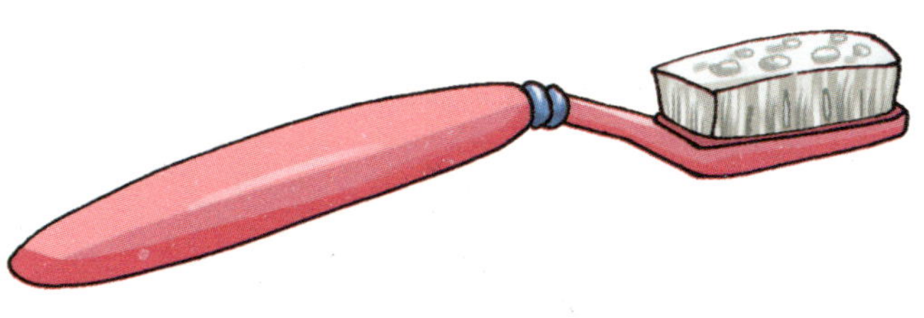

Heavy

In each box, write **H** for the picture that shows **heavy**.

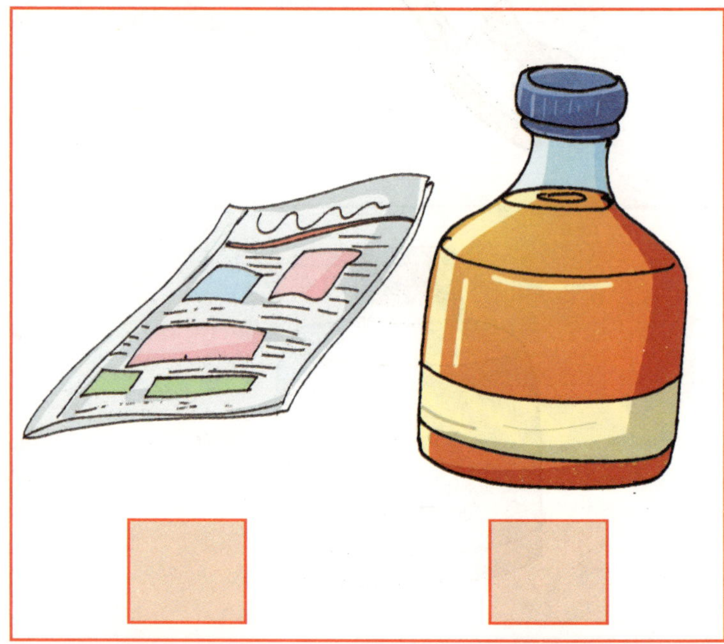

Light

In each box, write **L** for the picture that shows **light**.

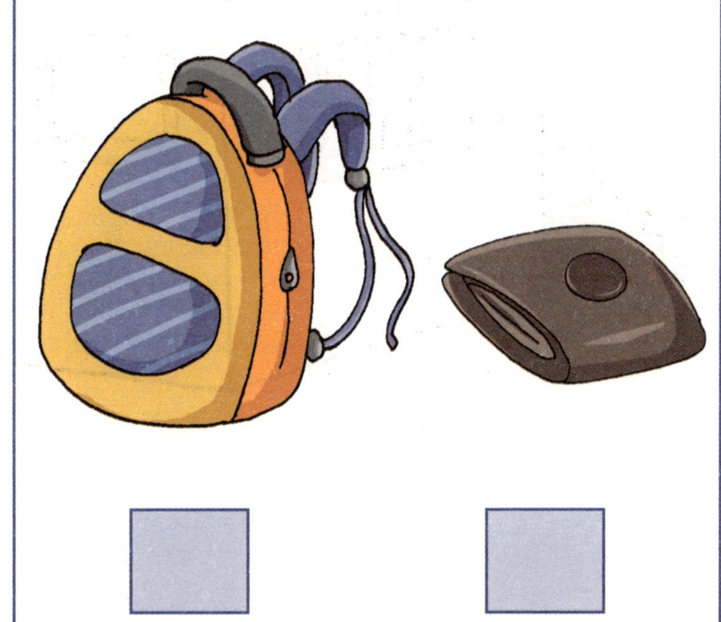

Up

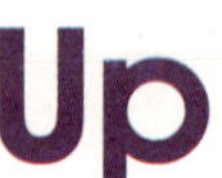

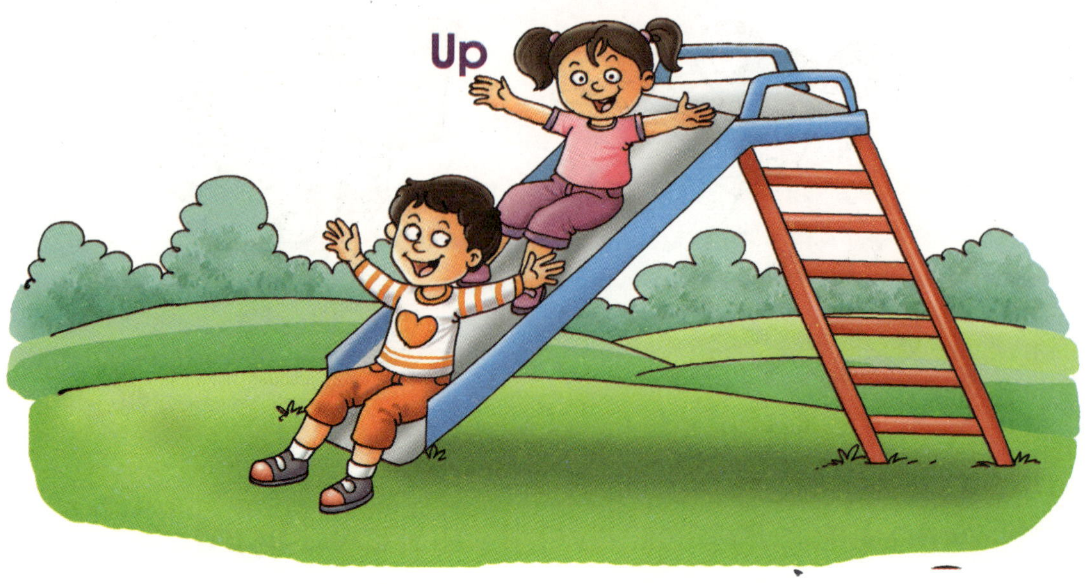

Circle (O) the one that is **up**.

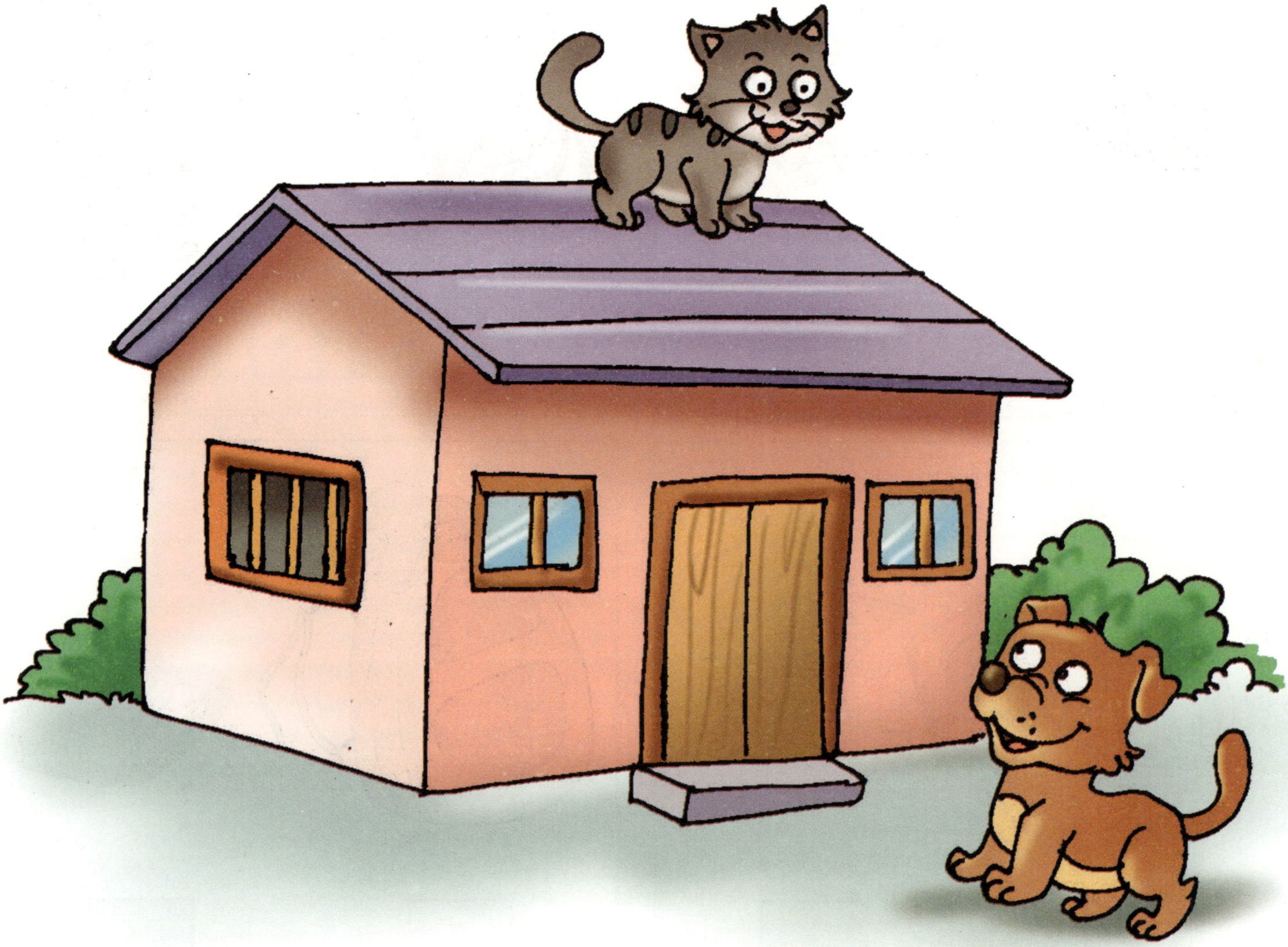

Down

Circle (O) the one that is **down**.

Near

Put a circle (O) around all the things that are **near** the tree.

Far

Far

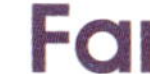

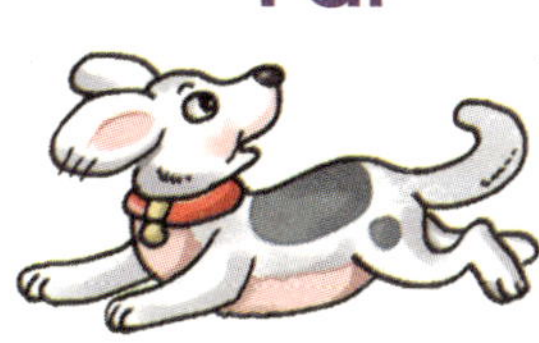

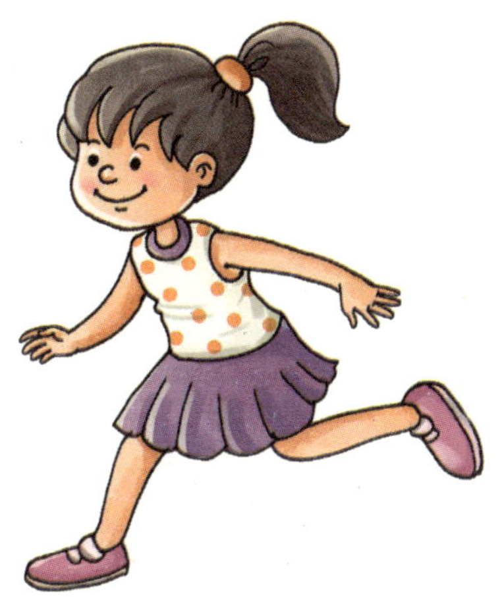

Cross (×) the animals that are **far** from the finish line.

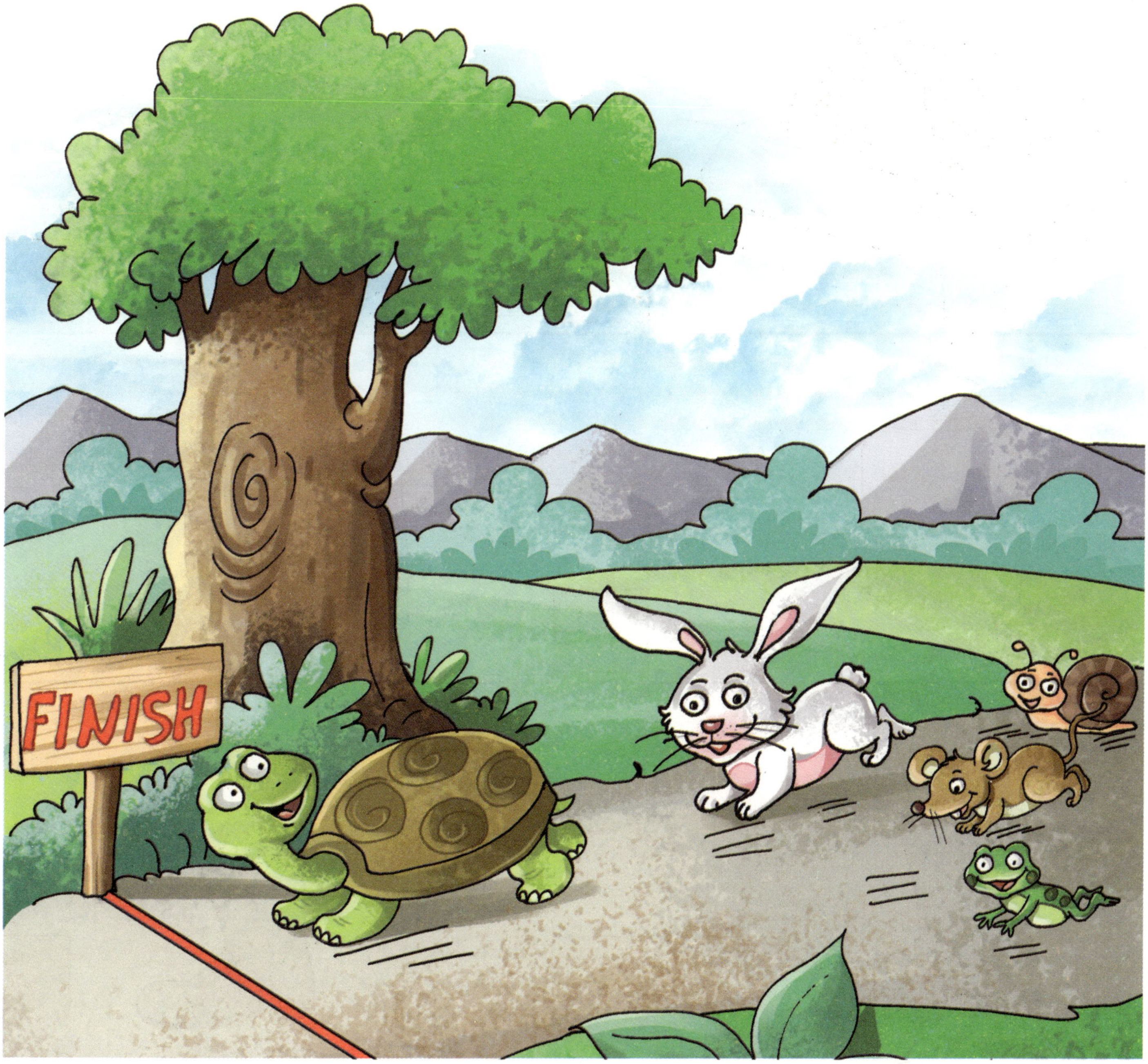

In

Tick (✓) the picture that shows **in**.

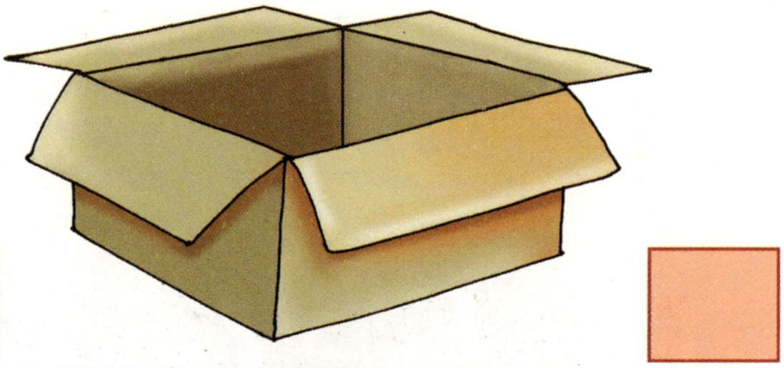

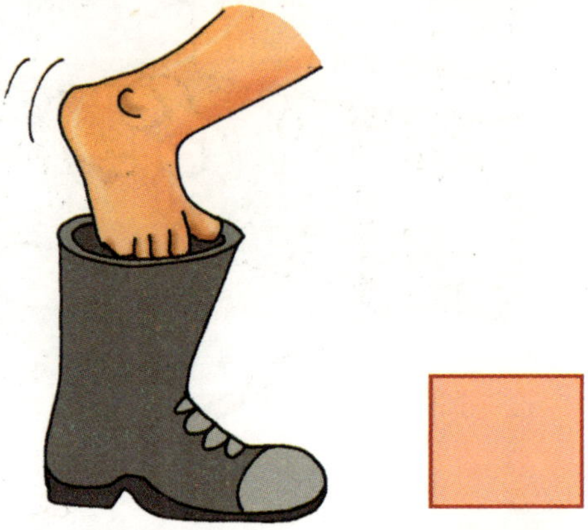

Out

Circle (O) the correct one that matches the card.

Same

These are **same**.

Circle (O) the picture that is the **same** as the first one.

Different

This is **different**.

Tick (✓)the picture that is **different** in each group.

Sorting Based On Colour

In each row, tick (✓) the pictures that are of **same colour** as the **first** one.

Sorting Based On Colour

Circle (O) the fish that are the **same colour** as the fisherman's **T-shirt**.

Sorting Based On Shape

Sort these scattered buttons.
Tick (✓) the **star** shaped buttons.
Cross (×) the **circle** shaped buttons.

Sorting Based On Shape

Sort the cards given below.
Tick (✓) all the **rectangles**.
Cross (×) the **triangles**.

Sorting Based On Size

Circle (O) the picture in each row that is of the **same size** as the first one.

More

The s are **more**.

Match one-to-one. Then circle (O) the group that has **more**.

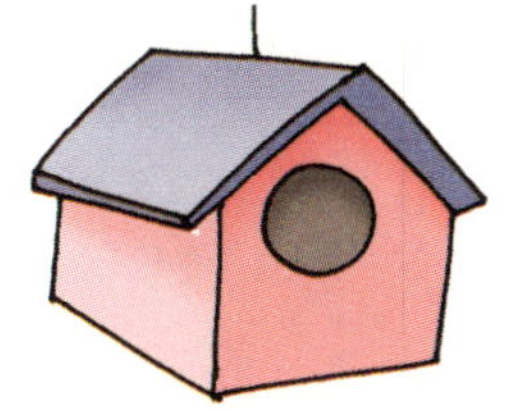 

Less

The [shirt]s are **less**.

Match one-to-one. Circle (O) the group that has **less**.

Many

This group has **many** crayons.

Circle (O) the group that has **many**.

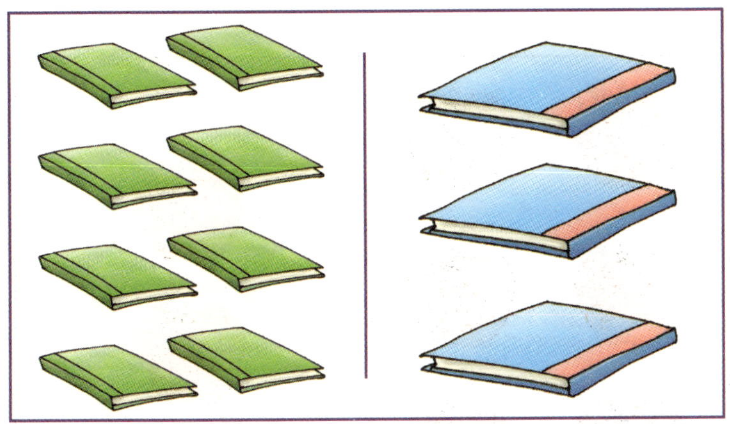

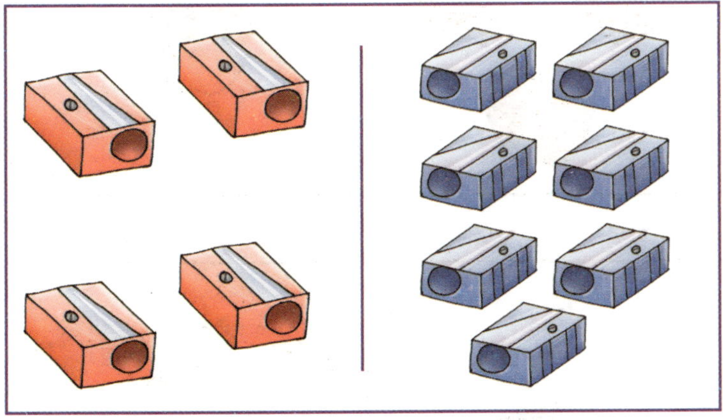

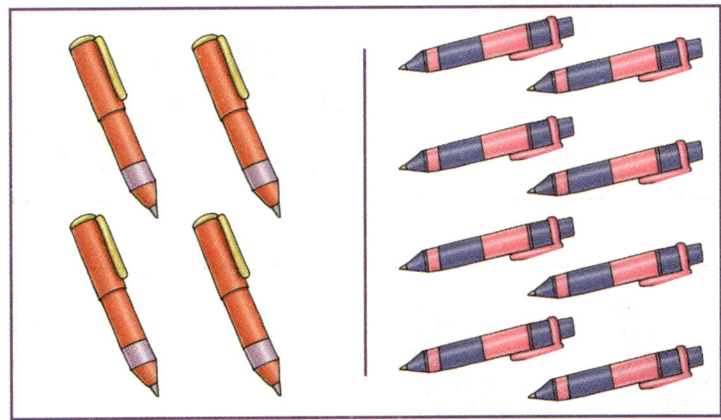

Few

This group has **few** strawberries.

Circle (O) the group that has **few**.

None

This group shows **none**.

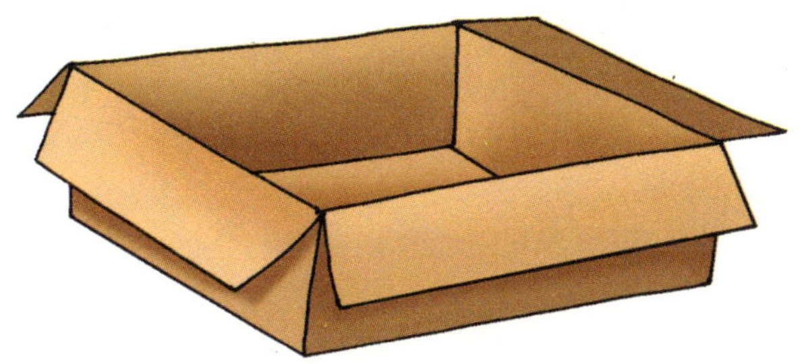

Tick (✓) the box that shows **none**.

Answer Key

Page 2
Page 3
Page 4
Page 5
Page 6
Page 7
Page 8
Page 9
Page 10
H
H
H
H
Page 11
L
L
L
L
Page 12

Answer Key

Page 13

Page 14

Page 15

Page 16

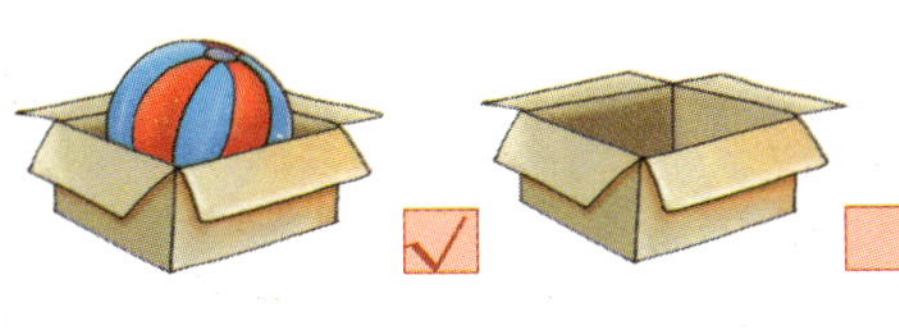

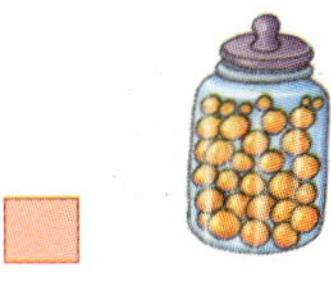

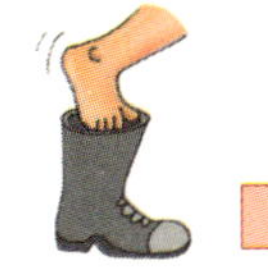

Page 17

Page 18

Page 19

Page 20

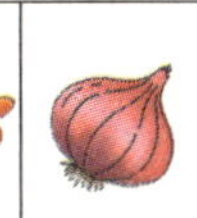

Page 21

Answer Key

Page 22

Page 25

Page 28

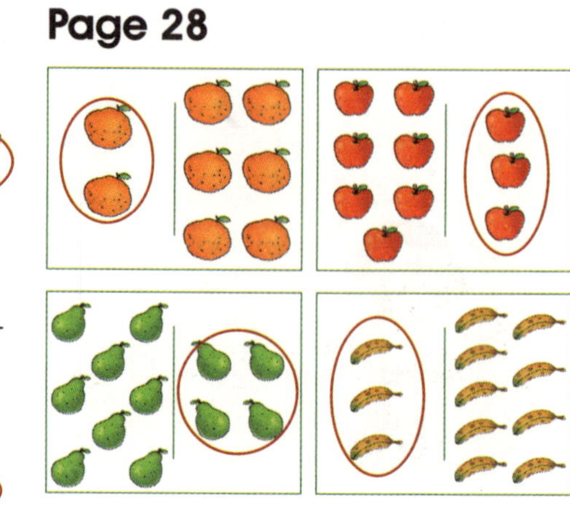

Page 23

Page 26

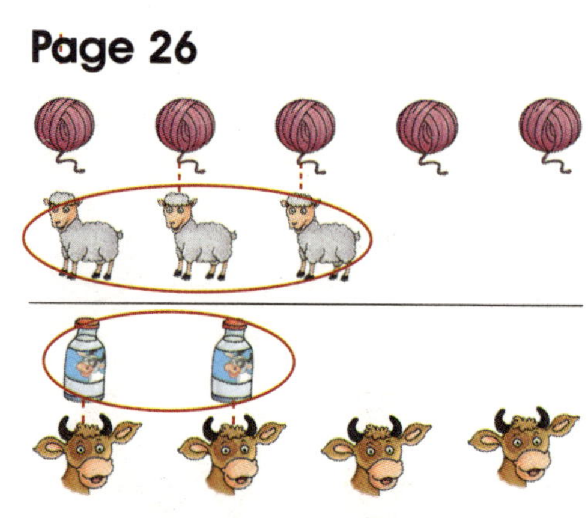

Page 29

Page 24

Page 27

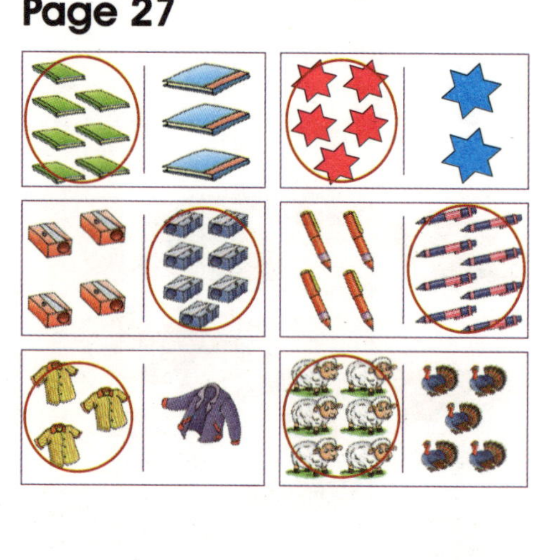